21st
Century
Skills Library

GLOBAL PRODUCTS

PENCILS

Kevin Cunningham

Cherry Lake Publishing
Ann Arbor, Michigan

Published in the United States of America by Cherry Lake Publishing
Ann Arbor, MI
www.cherrylakepublishing.com

Content Adviser: Charles Berolzheimer, President, California Cedar Products Company, Stockton, California

Photo Credits: Cover and page 1, © iStockphoto.com/CapturedNuance; page 4, © Christoffer Vika, used under license from Shutterstock, Inc.; pages 6, 9, 10, 14, 17, and 21, Courtesy of Faber-Castell; page 12, © iStockphoto.com/redmal; page 16, © prism_68, used under license from Shutterstock, Inc.; page 18, © Sally Scott, used under license from Shutterstock, Inc.; page 22, Courtesy of California Cedar Products Company; page 23, © iStockphoto.com/htjostheim; page 24, © Eric Gevaert, used under license from Shutterstock, Inc.; page 27, © Christian Lagerek, used under license from Shutterstock, Inc.

Map by XNR Productions Inc.

Library of Congress Cataloging-in-Publication Data
Cunningham, Kevin, 1966–
Pencils / by Kevin Cunningham.
   p. cm.—(Global products)
ISBN-13: 978-1-60279-122-0
ISBN-10: 1-60279-122-8
1. Pencils—Juvenile literature. I. Title. II. Series.
TS1268.C96 2008
674'.88—dc22   2007034976

Cherry Lake Publishing would like to acknowledge the work of
The Partnership for 21st Century Skills.
Please visit www.21stcenturyskills.org for more information.

TABLE OF CONTENTS

CHAPTER ONE

LEAVING A MARK ON HISTORY

Carpenter's pencils have two wide flat sides so they won't roll off of flat surfaces.

Dai showed the stub of her pencil to her friend Gretchen. "It's too short," she said.

Gretchen looked around the house for another one. As she wondered where else to search, she heard the whine from her father's saw out in the garage. She suggested they go ask him about a new pencil. Gretchen's father, Lars, noticed them and shut off the saw. The garage smelled like sawdust and oil.

"Do you have a pencil?" Gretchen said.

"All I have is a carpenter's pencil," her father said.

"What's that?" Dai asked. He handed her a pencil with a dull tip. It had two wide, flat sides and two narrow, flat sides.

"Why does it look so funny?" Dai asked as she examined the pencil.

"The same reason the pencils you use have six sides. So it doesn't roll off the table."

"Ahhhh," Gretchen and Dai said together.

"The pencil is an amazing invention," Lars said. "Before it came along—"

"Wait," Gretchen said. "There weren't always pencils?"

"No," Lars said. "Pencils were invented about five hundred years ago."

"Were they like our pencils?" Dai asked.

Lars thought for a second. "In some ways they were, and in some ways they weren't."

In the 1500s, miners near the town of Keswick, in England's rolling Cumberland Mountains, found a gray mineral that smudged onto their fingers. The substance turned out to be a soft kind of rock. Sheepherders

This graphite will be ground into powder before being used to make pencil lead.

in the region named rough chunks of the mineral "marking stones." They used it to mark their livestock.

The substance had another use, too. It left a mark on paper as tiny flakes of the mineral clung to the paper's fibers. The English shaped pieces of the stone into sticks and wrapped the sticks in string. Hollowed-out wooden sticks soon replaced string. The pencil was born.

For a long time, the mineral was thought to be a kind of **lead**, but it turned out to be a new substance. Two centuries after the Keswick discovery, chemists took the Greek word *graphien*, meaning "to write," and named the mineral **graphite**. The term lead stuck, though. People still use it today to describe the inside of a pencil even though it's inaccurate.

In the 1700s, a German cabinetmaker named Kaspar Faber cut long, thin pieces of wood in half and shaped a groove in the wood. Then he put a stick of graphite inside and glued the wood halves together. But his pencils were not as good as British pencils. The graphite he used had less carbon and didn't mark as well. It was good enough for marking a barrel, but not something an artist would use. Frenchman Nicolas-Jacques Conté and Austrian Josef Hardtmuth laid the groundwork for solving that problem.

Conté took out a **patent** in 1795 on a process to mix graphite with clay and water. Once the mixture was molded into sticks, Conté baked them in a furnace. A manufacturer using this process could make more pencils at lower cost because he needed less graphite.

Kaspar Faber's great-grandson Lothar von Faber added to Conté's and Hardtmuth's work. By mixing different amounts of clay with the graphite, Lothar turned out pencils able to make thicker, darker lines (a mixture with more graphite) or thinner, lighter lines (a mixture with more clay). The system he invented for different pencils is still used today.

Lothar von Faber's factories sawed lumber, cut wooden slats, and then made rounded grooves in the pencil's wood. The machines turned out pieces of wood that were all exactly the same. The slats were cut to take rounded graphite rods, rather than the square-shaped "leads" popular in earlier years. These improvements helped workers make more pencils in less time for less money.

Lothar von Faber had one more idea. He put his company's name on each pencil. As a result, the Faber pencil became one of the first **brand-name** products.

Eventually, the old Keswick mines ran out of graphite. Pencil manufacturers had to search for a new graphite source. In the mid-1800s, Jean-Pierre Alibert, a French adventurer, found a new graphite mine. The bad news: it was on a mountaintop in distant Siberia. Lothar von Faber agreed to buy graphite from Alibert. Siberian miners dug it out of the ground. Reindeer hauled it across the country to ports. Ships carried it to European pencil factories. In Germany, Faber's employees combined it with clay from Bavaria.

People in the United States bought foreign-made pencils until 1812. That year, William Munroe started a pencil manufacturing company in Massachusetts. Munroe didn't bake the graphite and clay mixture. Instead, he developed a graphite paste that didn't require a furnace. Another early U.S pencil manufacturer was author Henry David Thoreau, who also had a factory in Massachusetts.

Lothar von Faber was Kaspar Faber's great-grandson.

Pencil manufacturing became a big business in the United States during the Civil War (1861–1865). The Union Army passed out thousands of pencils to soldiers for writing letters and keeping journals. Eberhard Faber, Lothar's brother, moved to the United States and opened the country's

Eberhard Faber opened the first mechanized pencil factory in the United States in 1861.

first **mechanized** pencil factory in New York City in 1861. Other German producers soon followed Faber to North America. They opened factories in the United States to take advantage of the growing market. Americans were using more than twenty million pencils per year in the 1870s. The pencil was on its way to becoming a global product.

CHAPTER TWO

GRAPHITE

"Is the graphite in a pencil at least related to lead?" Gretchen asked.

"No," responded Lars, "but there are minerals that are close to graphite. One is diamond. The other is coal. Even though all three materials are related, they're very different. For instance, diamond is the hardest known mineral, while graphite is one of the softest."

"And we don't make pencils out of diamonds," Gretchen said.

"That'd be expensive," Dai said.

"True," Lars replied. "But graphite is valuable in its own way. People use it for much more than pencils."

࿇

Graphite's combination of light weight and strength make it excellent for products such as golf clubs. Battery-makers have used graphite for years because it conducts electricity. The material is used in hybrid car fuel cells for similar reasons. Graphite is an important ingredient in some kinds of paint because it is water-resistant.

Though graphite is found in many countries, the major producers are China (by far the biggest), Mexico, India, Canada, Brazil, and North Korea. China and Mexico have the largest graphite **reserves**—that is, the amount of the material still left in the ground.

Pencils are just one product made with graphite.
Some golf clubs also contain graphite.

Three kinds of natural graphite are mined. **Amorphous graphite** is often found mixed with coal or slate. It traditionally provided the graphite for pencils. Mexico extracts significant amounts of amorphous graphite. Other deposits are located in Austria, the Czech Republic, and the Korean peninsula.

Sri Lanka leads the world in mining **crystalline graphite** (also called lumpy graphite). Graphite there appears as veins of rock. The veins might be as narrow as a centimeter or as wide as a meter or more. The Sri Lankan companies Kahatagaha Graphite Lanka, Ltd., and Bogala Graphite Lanka, Ltd., operate two of the world's largest graphite mines.

Found around the world, **flake graphite** is the most common type. It occurs as tiny crystals. Flake graphite conducts heat and electricity extremely well. This makes it good for many engineering uses. China mines the most flake graphite. India and Mozambique are also major producers. It is also possible to make synthetic (man-made) graphite in factories using petroleum and coal products.

Companies mine graphite in two ways. The first is by digging shafts into the earth. Workers dig out the mineral with machinery or hand tools. Underground mines are common in Sri Lanka but also can be found in Mexico and other countries.

Surface mining is the second and more common way to mine graphite. Bulldozers, shovels, and other digging machines remove the topsoil to expose the rock. Open pits are dug to get at deposits deeper in the ground. Graphite is a soft mineral and doesn't need to be blasted by explosives to remove it from the earth.

A graphite company like iCarbon of Delano, Pennsylvania, is a good example of how a single corporation reaches around the world. iCarbon operates two mines in China and others in Madagascar and Ontario, Canada. Two manufacturing plants in the United States and Chenzhou, China, process the mined graphite. Warehouses in the United States and Paris, France, store it for sale to manufacturers that make products such as fuel cells and golf clubs—and, of course, pencils.

What are some of the reasons a company would have locations in different countries? What are the advantages and disadvantages of having locations in more than one country?

CHAPTER THREE

ROCKS INTO WRITING

Graphite, clay, and water are mixed into a thick paste that will be used to make pencil lead.

Dai rubbed her thumb over the dull lead at the end of her pencil stub. "So the graphite comes out of the ground?"

"That's right," Lars replied. "But there's more to a pencil than just raw graphite. Companies first have to do something called refining. They apply heat and acids to the raw graphite. That strips out the other kinds of rock mixed in with the graphite."

∾

Sanford, a Bellwood, Illinois, company, operates a pencil factory in Lewisburg, Tennessee. The initial step there is to create the material for the pencil lead. The process hasn't changed much since the days of Conté and Hardtmuth. Sanford workers add water to graphite and clay. The mixture is crushed in a drum for two or three days. High pressure squeezes the water from the mixture and it is left to dry.

Then a mixing machine's powerful arms stir the right amount of water into the mixture until it becomes a thick, gray paste.

Another machine, called an extruder, forces the paste through a hole. The hole shapes the paste into spaghetti-like strands. Cutting tools chop the strands into pieces roughly the length of a pencil. These leads, or cores, are collected into batches shaped like bricks.

21st Century Content

Though it was founded in 1857, Sanford only started making pens and markers after World War II. Sanford has since expanded its business by purchasing its competitors. For example, in 1994, the company bought Eberhard Faber USA, the famous pencil-maker founded during the Civil War. Six years later it added Paper Mate, known for its pens.

Such purchases, known as acquisitions, are a common way for a company to add to its product lines. Sanford itself was bought by the Newell Company (now known as Newell Rubbermaid) in 1992. Newell Rubbermaid is a huge corporation that sells products ranging from windows to hardware to toys. Sanford is one of the largest divisions of Newell Rubbermaid.

Companies are often looking for new products. For example, some pencil manufacturers make colored pencils. Someone had to come up with a process to create the new product. To make colored pencils, workers combine clay, pigment, and wax into the material that makes up the color core. Someone, or some group of people, had to figure out that this was the best mixture for the color core.

Imagine that you were the person who came up with the idea of making colored pencils. Your boss tells you to work with a team of people to develop your idea. How would you convince other people that colored pencils were a good idea and that they should be on your team? What would you do to get people working together to bring your idea to life?

A furnace bakes the cores for twenty-four hours or more at temperatures of 1800 degrees Fahrenheit (982 degrees Celsius). The heat causes the water to boil off and helps the graphite and clay bind together. Once removed from the oven, the cores are cooled. It's then that the pencil's other major component, wood, comes into play.

Many pencil manufacturers also make colored pencils.

CHAPTER FOUR

MAKING THE PENCIL

*A Faber-Castell employee holds wood slats
that will be used to make pencils.*

Gretchen picked up a wooden board. "You have wood," she exclaimed.

"You could make us a pencil!"

"I don't know how to make pencils," Lars said.

"You make tables and chairs."

"But I don't have pencil-making machines."

Wood from cedars and other trees is used to make pencils.

"Machines?" said Dai. "I thought they just took a little piece of wood and drilled a hole in it to put in the lead."

"That's how it seems it might be," Lars said, "but it doesn't work that way."

Wood for pencils cannot shrink or warp due to changes in temperature. And it has to be strong so the pencil doesn't splinter or crack when it is sharpened. Cedar wood fits this description.

In the 1800s, U.S. pencil manufacturers preferred wood from the eastern red cedar. Today, the incense-cedar of Oregon and California is used to make high-quality pencils. A single tree can provide wood for about 170,000 pencils.

Companies such as Sierra Pacific Industries and Soper-Wheeler in California manage forests of incense-cedar so that more trees are planted than cut down. That guarantees the availability of the wood in future years.

These companies produce a lumber product called pencil stock in their sawmills. The pencil stock is shipped overseas to manufacturers, such as the California Cedar Products Company factory in Tianjin, China.

Workers in California Cedar's Tianjin plant cut the incense-cedar into slats. Each slat forms half of the wood that sandwiches a length of graphite to make a group of pencils. Slats are approximately 7.25 inches (18.4 centimeters) in length. The width of the slat determines the number of pencils it will make. Machines cut semicircular grooves in the slat. Each groove is half of the diameter of a graphite core. The slats are treated with a mixture of wax and a stain that colors them. Then they are dried in a kiln for several days.

Slats made in Tianjin are sold and sent to pencil factories in many countries. Sanford's Lewisburg facility has one of the world's most

automated processes for producing wooden pencils. There, from the time slats are loaded into the first machine until the finished pencil is ready to be packaged, they are rarely touched by human hands. In the first step, machines cut grooves into each slat. The grooves are semicircles half the diameter of a graphite core. Next, the grooved slats transfer down a conveyor belt, where a second machine coats half of them with glue and rolls one lead into each groove.

Then the machine surrounds the core with wood by placing a matching slat onto the first slat, like a sandwich. The slat sandwiches transfer to a wheel clamp machine that presses them together until the glue sets. As each clamp of sandwiches dries, it unloads into a new conveyor that feeds the sandwiches to a shaper machine.

In the shaper, sharp-edged cutting tools above and below the sandwich shape the wood into individual pencils. The raw wood pencils continue down the conveyor belt for the final touches. They

A machine inserts lead into pencil slats.

accumulate in a feeding bin. From there they are pushed through a gasket at the bottom of a paint vat and are covered with a clear coating known as lacquer. The pencils dry on the conveyor belt and get several more coats of lacquer. Then a foil-stamping machine impresses the all-important brand name onto the pencil.

A machine attaches ferrules and erasers to pencils.

Attaching the eraser is the final step in the pencil-making process. The eraser sits in a metal holder called a ferrule. Machines fasten the ferrule onto a pencil end with glue or by clamping it on. The eraser slides down a tube into a waiting ferrule and a machine squeezes the metal around the eraser to hold it in place.

Workers use machines to put the finished pencils into packages. The packages go into boxes and the boxes go onto movable platforms called **pallets**. The pencils are now ready for shipment to stores.

CHAPTER FIVE

THE SUPPLY CHAIN

ars, Gretchen, and Dai hopped into the truck to go to the store to buy a pack of pencils. On the way, Dai tried to figure out how pencils made in a factory got to the drugstore near her neighborhood.

"Is there a pencil factory close to where we live?" she asked.

"No," Lars said.

"How does the store get pencils, then?"

As he drove, Lars explained how it happened.

Products are stacked on pallets in a warehouse. Pallets make it easier to move many boxes at one time.

A truck backs up to a loading dock at a factory.

Pencils are loaded onto trucks at factory loading docks. Where do trucks take their loads? Some pencils go to **wholesalers** who buy up large amounts of product, raise the price, and sell it at a profit to their own customers. Examples of wholesalers include office-supply companies, small businesses, and individuals who sell office supplies on the Internet.

Other pencils are sold to big retail store chains such as OfficeMax, Target, and Wal-Mart, and are delivered to their huge regional warehouses. Each warehouse serves a group of stores in a geographic territory. Regular shipments of pencils and other products are sent from these warehouses to individual stores. The size of a shipment depends on the product's sales history at a store, the time of year (many pencils are sold in August and September when kids go back to school), and other factors.

The network of manufacturers, transportation companies, storage facilities, distribution centers, retail stores, and customers is often referred to as a distribution **supply chain**. Pencils made overseas face a supply-chain complication. These products have to be shipped over long distances. China's pencil manufacturers, for example, made approximately 10 billion pencils in 2004. To get the pencils to consumers in North America, Chinese companies need a supply chain capable of stretching across whole oceans. That's where containerships come in.

Containerships are an important part of the global economy. Close to 8,000 of them sail the world's oceans hauling containers full of goods. Containers can be stacked close together and workers quickly move them on and off ships. Even a big containership usually can be unloaded in just a matter of hours.

How do large retailers keep track of how many pencils (and other products) they sell? How do they make sure that they have the products that people want to buy in stock at their stores? They use computerized tracking systems. These systems speed up the way products move through the supply chain. When a cashier scans an item at the store, a computer system keeps track of how much of that item is left in the store. The system helps managers know when to order more of a certain item. It may even be programmed to automatically place orders with suppliers when the store supply of a product gets low. Computer systems help stores make sure that they almost always have items in stock. And that means happier customers and more sales.

Harbor pilots and other workers spring into action when containerships enter a harbor.

Shipments of pencils made in China travel to North America in containers on containerships. The journey across the Pacific Ocean takes about two weeks, depending on the weather and other factors. The containerships dock at one of the

West Coast's major ports, such as Long Beach, California, or Seattle, Washington. As a ship nears port, a harbor pilot—someone skilled in guiding large ships safely through a harbor's obstacles to the dock—is ferried out on a small boat to meet it. When the containership docks safely, workers leap into action with forklifts and cranes.

The pencils continue on their supply-chain journey. Trucks carry them to warehouses and distributors. It takes just a few weeks for pencils manufactured in China to arrive at your neighborhood store.

Gretchen and Dai took a package of pencils off the store shelf and looked it over carefully. "I never realized that pencils were made from parts that come from around the world," said Dai.

"I know," said Gretchen. "Graphite from Mexico and clay from the United States."

"Don't forget the wood harvested by loggers in Oregon or California!" Dai replied.

"And all those workers in China preparing the wood slats. And other workers putting the pencils together, maybe right here in the United States," Gretchen's father added. "Even though the pencil seems as simple as always, the truth is that the global economy has transformed every part of it."

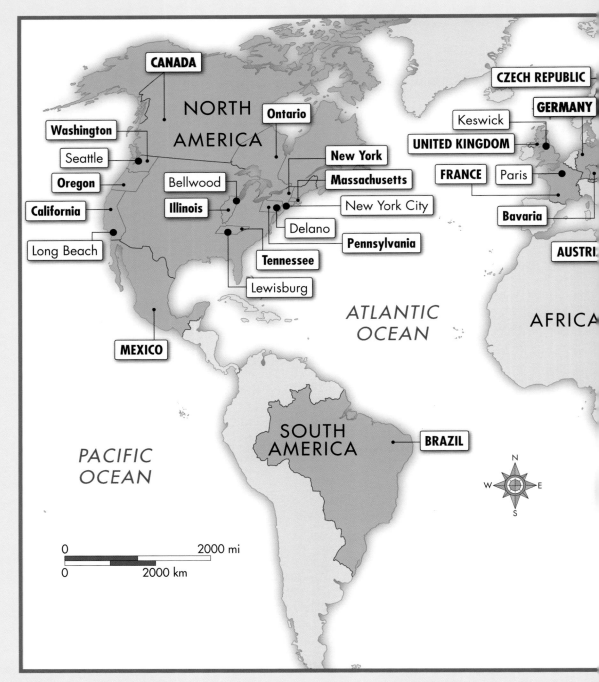

This map shows the countries and cities mentioned in the tex

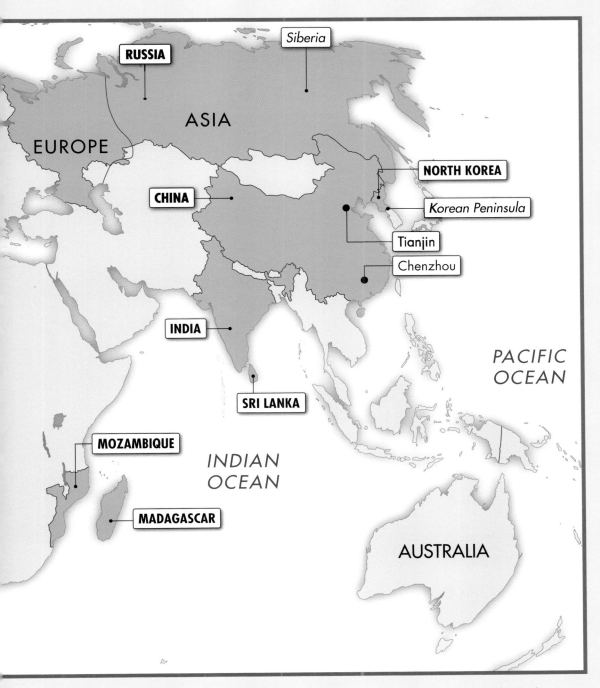

They are the locations of some of the companies involved in the making and selling of pencils.

GLOSSARY

acquisitions (a-kwuh-ZIH-shunz) things that have been newly gained, or acquired

amorphous graphite (uh-MOR-fus GRAF-ite) a kind of graphite often found mixed with coal or slate; it is commonly used in pencils

brand name (BRAND NAME) a specific product name that is identified with a specific company, intended to make consumers loyal to the brand so that they keep buying it and related products; Ticonderoga and Faber are well-known pencil brand names

crystalline graphite (KRISS-tuh-lin GRAF-ite) a kind of graphite that appears in veins, sometimes called lumpy graphite

flake graphite (FLAYK GRAF-ite) the most common type of graphite, it is found as tiny crystals and is a good conductor of heat and electricity

graphite (GRAF-ite) a soft, black mineral

lead (LED) a heavy metal

mechanized (MEK-uh-nizd) equipped with machinery

pallets (PAL-uhts) portable platforms for moving and storing materials

patent (PAT-uhnt) the legal document giving an inventor the sole right to make and sell an item he or she invented

reserves (rih-ZURVZ) the amount of a mineral still left in the ground and available to be mined or extracted

supply chain (suh-PLYE CHAYN) a network of workers, suppliers, and transportation that connects raw materials to manufacturers and manufacturers to people who wish to buy a finished product

wholesalers (HOL-say-lurs) individuals who or companies that buy a product in large amounts from a manufacturer and resell it

FOR MORE INFORMATION

Books

Green, Jen. *China*. Washington, DC: National Geographic, 2006.

Royston, Angela. *How Is a Pencil Made?* Chicago: Heinemann, 2005.

Web Sites

Cumberland Pencil Museum
www.pencilmuseum.co.uk
Learn about the pencil museum located in historic Keswick in the United Kingdom.

Facts About Pencils
www.pencilfacts.com
Watch videos to learn more about how pencils are made.

The Pencil Pages!
www.pencils.com
Information on pencil history and pencil making along with a
trivia page, sponsored by the Incense Cedar Institute.

INDEX

ABOUT THE AUTHOR

Kevin Cunningham is the author of several books, including biographies of Joseph Stalin and J. Edgar Hoover and a series on diseases in human history. He lives in Chicago.